Alphabet Boats

Samantha R. Vamos

Illustrated by **Ryan O'Rourke**

ABCDEFGHIJKLMNOPQRSTUVWXYZ

Charlesbridge

Raise the anchor.
Grab the oars.
Chart a course
to distant shores.

A is for airboat.
Its flat hull skims glade and shoal.

B is for barge,
hauling freight such as coal.

C is for catamaran,
with stability and speed.

D is for dory.
Cast a line where fish feed.

E is for electric boat—
solar powered to take a trip.

F is for fireboat,
fighting fires on shore and ship.

G is for gondola.
Cruise the Grand Canal
propelled by oar.

H is for houseboat,
a motorized home to
move or moor.

I is for iceboat.
Race along on runners or skis.

J is for jet boat.
It maneuvers with ease.

K is for kayak,
long and narrow
to move faster.

L is for lifeboat—
rescue in case
of disaster.

M is for motorboat,
a high-speed thrill ride.

N is for narrow boat, just seven feet wide.

O is for outrigger canoe,
with support float on the side.

P is for punt.
Wield a pole and gently glide.

P p

Q is for Q-boat,
an armed merchant ship.

R is for racing shell.
Row and coast at a clip.

S is for submarine,
patrolling under the ocean.

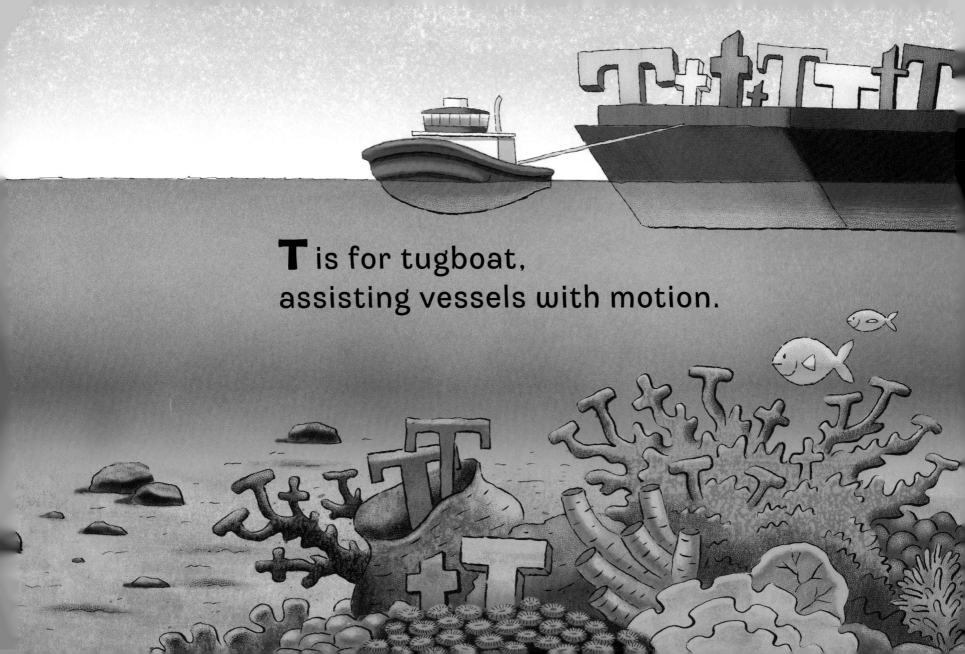

T is for tugboat,
assisting vessels with motion.

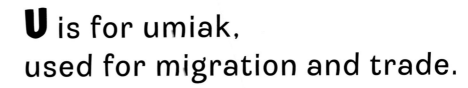

U is for umiak,
used for migration and trade.

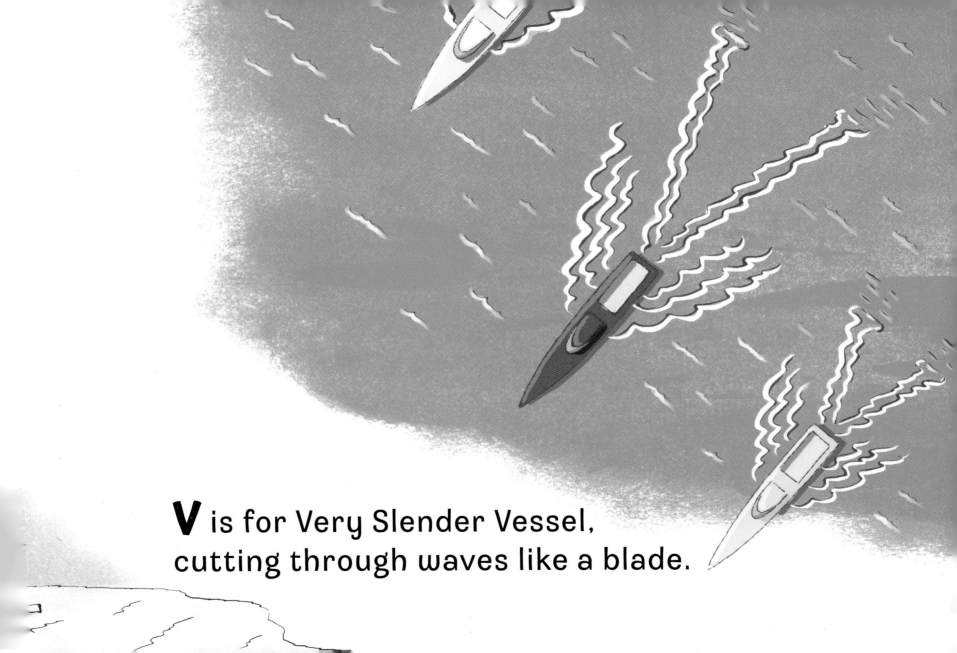

V is for Very Slender Vessel,
cutting through waves like a blade.

W is for water taxi—
commute or tour, boats to hail.

X is for X boat,
to teach beginners to sail.

Y is for yacht—
private, elegant,
and vast.

Z is for zebec,
a merchant ship,
light and fast.

Traveling far
from shore to sea,
boats work hard
from A to Z!

Cast off!
Set sail!
Splash!

Alphabet boats.

An **airboat** has a flat-bottomed hull that skims the water's surface. Its engine and propeller are mounted on deck; the propeller pushes air behind the boat to propel it forward.

A **barge** is a large flat-bottomed boat that moves heavy cargo. Some barges have engines, while others are pushed or pulled by tugboats.

A **catamaran** has two connected hulls that create stability. Most catamarans have sails and twin engines. Catamarans are used for racing and recreation.

A **dory** is a small flat-bottomed boat with flared sides and a pointed bow. Dories have been popular fishing boats for centuries. They may also be rigged to sail.

An **electric boat** is powered by electricity. Some have solar panels to convert sunlight into energy that is stored in batteries and used to power the motor.

A **fireboat** pulls water from the ocean, lake, or river below it. Fireboats fight fires on ships, docks, and near shore.

A **gondola** is a long, narrow flat-bottomed boat with a curved stern and prow. Gondoliers use a long, thin oar to propel and steer these boats on canals in Venice, Italy, famous for its gondolas.

A **houseboat** is a motorized boat used primarily as a home. Houseboats usually stay moored to a dock. They are typically found on calm water and aren't generally considered ocean-worthy.

Iceboats sail and race over frozen lakes and bays. The ice must be smooth and several inches thick to be safe for iceboating. The boat's hull is fitted with skis or skates called runners.

A **jet boat** is powered by water drawn from under its hull and expelled from its stern. Jet boats are speedy and highly maneuverable.

A **kayak** is a slim boat with pointed ends and a cockpit that seats one or two paddlers. A paddle with a blade at each end allows for speed, balance, and control.

A **lifeboat** is a rescue boat often carried on larger ships. Propelled by oars or powered by a sail or an engine, lifeboats can be inflatable and may include emergency supplies.

A **motorboat** (also called speedboat or powerboat) is powered by an engine. Motorboats vary in size and design and are used for cruising, fishing, and water sports.

A **narrow boat** must be less than seven feet wide to pass through British canals. Originally horse-drawn cargo boats, narrow boats are now used for recreation or as homes and usually have an engine.

An **outrigger canoe** has a float attached to one or both sides. The float supports and stabilizes the canoe. Outrigger canoes are used for surfing, fishing, and racing.

A **punt** is a flat-bottomed boat with square ends and straight sides. Punts are used in shallow water and are propelled by a pole. Originally used for cargo and fishing, punts are now used for fishing, racing, and leisure.

A **Q-boat** was a decoy ship used during World Wars I and II. Disguised as a merchant ship to lure enemy submarines to the surface, the Q-boat fired its hidden weapons once the submarines were within attack range.

A **racing shell** is a long, narrow rowing boat with sliding seats and long oars.

A **submarine** is shaped like a cylinder and can stay under water for long periods of time. Submarines vary in size, and some operate remotely.

A **tugboat** tows or pushes vessels such as ships and barges through harbors, canals, rivers, or the ocean. Some tugboats help break ice or assist with firefighting.

An **umiak** is a boat made of animal hides stretched over wood. Umiaks have traditionally been used by Inuit and Yupik indigenous people for transportation, hunting, and fishing. Today people use motorized boats with a similar construction.

A **Very Slender Vessel** (VSV) has a slim, sharp bow that pierces through waves instead of bouncing over them, creating a comfortable and safe ride at very high speeds. The VSV was originally developed for use by military forces.

A **water taxi** can operate on a schedule or by demand. While many types of boats are used as taxis, they all have the same job: transporting passengers from one place to another.

An **X boat** is a lightweight, fast sailboat for beginners. It has two sails—the jib and mainsail—and is ideal for lakes and rivers.

A **yacht** is for cruising and racing and uses sails or a motor. Yachts are sometimes luxurious and exceptionally large.

A **zebec** was a Mediterranean sailing ship with an overhanging bow and stern, two or three masts, and oars. It was used for war and commerce in the 1700s and 1800s.

A B C D E F G H I J K L M N O P Q R S T U V W X Y Z

For Greg with love always. (H. P.)
And for Jennifer Simms and Jackson with love.
—S. R. V.

To my dad, for always driving the boat.
—R. O.

Published by Charlesbridge
85 Main Street
Watertown, MA 02472
(617) 926-0329
www.charlesbridge.com

Library of Congress Cataloging-in-Publication Data
Names: Vamos, Samantha R., author. | O'Rourke, Ryan, illustrator.
Title: Alphabet boats / Samantha R. Vamos; illustrated by Ryan O'Rourke.
Description: Watertown, MA: Charlesbridge, [2018]
Identifiers: LCCN 2016053952 (print) | LCCN 2016058871 (ebook) | ISBN
    9781580897310 (reinforced for library use) | ISBN 9781607349778
    (ebook) | ISBN 9781607349785 (ebook pdf)
Subjects: LCSH: Boats and boating—Juvenile literature. | English
    language—Alphabet—Juvenile literature. | Alphabet books.
Classification: LCC GV775.3 .V36 2018 (print) | LCC GV775.3 (ebook) | DDC
    623.82—dc23
LC record available at https://lccn.loc.gov/2016053952

PZ8.3.V32537Aln 2015
[E]—dc23   2014010487

Printed in China
(hc) 10 9 8 7 6 5 4 3 2 1

Illustrations done in Adobe Photoshop
Display type set in Chaloops by Chank Co.
Text type set in Jesterday by Tjarda Koster-Jelloween
Color separations by Colourscan Print Co Pte Ltd, Singapore
Printed by 1010 Printing International Limited in Huizhou, Guangdong, China
Production supervision by Brian G. Walker
Designed by Diane M. Earley